MY GOD WE WILL PERISH

MY GOD WE WILL PERISH

Threat and Hope for the World in the Last Days

———◆———

PAUL ROMERO

MANYSEASONSPress
Mesa, Arizona • 2019

FIRST EDITION

My God We Will Perish, Threat and Hope for the World in the Last Days

Copyright © 2019 by Paul Romero

Scripture quotations taken from The Holy Bible, New International Version® NIV®
Copyright © 1973 1978 1984 2011 by Biblica, Inc. TM
Used by permission. All rights reserved worldwide.

Published by Many Seasons Press
(An Imprint of Multimedia Publishing Project)
PO Box 50553
Mesa, AZ 85208
480.939.9689 | MultimediaPublishingProject.com

Cover & book interior design by Yolie Hernandez (AZBookDesigner@icloud.com)

ISBN 13: 978-1-936885-31-2
All rights reserved, including the right of reproduction
in whole or in part in any form.

Printed in the United States of America.

Disclaimer: The opinions expressed in this work are those of the author(s) and do not necessarily reflect the opinions of Many Seasons Press (MSP).

DEDICATION

This book is dedicated to my Heavenly Father, my Lord, my God.

CONTENTS

Introduction.....ix

What is Earth?.....1

Genesis.....3

Adam.....5

Fall of Man.....7

Humans Succeed Fallen Angels.....9

The Great Flood.....11

Shem German's Root.....15

Who Are We?.....21

The Morning Star.....25

The Beginning of Civilization.....27

Truth is Fallen.....29

My God We Will Perish

Nuclear Arsenal.....31

The Two-Horned Beast.....33

A Deliverer.....37

World Crisis at the End.....41

The Second Adam.....43

The Love of God 45

Earth's Face in Devastation.....47

What Man Has Done.....49

The Prince of Darkness 53

He Wants Us Good.....57

The Language We Speak.....59

Hope.....61

INTRODUCTION

THE BIBLE, as interpreted by numerous scholars, philosophers and distinguished writers, is generally offered as a sacred text in the United States. It is hardly ever considered as a historical document. But the question remains: Who wrote its 66 books? Where were they written? And, what were its authors trying to do? Ministers, priests, pastors and lay people would prefer to avoid the crisis of faith that these questions might provoke. But as rational people, asking these questions is a good way to understand the Bible.

The Bible is full of paradoxes. To make sense of it we need to know who wrote it. It was written by men, not God. Equally important is why do the stories, particularly the Gospels, contradict each other. According to the Gospels of Mark and John, Jesus died on different days. Luke claims Jesus, in route to the cross, was calm. John says He performed miracles to prove His provenance. Matthew says He demurred. Most of the 27 books of the New Testament were written long after Christ's death, and only eight of them were actually written by the people initially credited as authors.

When the New Testament became canonical, there were many gospels floating around. Why did four endure but not others? The answers are all unclear but surely they reflect contemporary biases.

My God We Will Perish

To ordinary people, just the size of the Bible and its sheer length, along with its unique verses and fine printing, tend to have many ignore reading it altogether, and prefer listen to lectures from many knowledgeable individuals.

Contrary to the popular thought of many people, the Bible did not "descend from on high." It was created down here on earth. Despite this fact, many people maintain their faith. Belief is not just doctrine. It can also tell us how to live and love.

What	*Earth*
Who	*Firmament*
When	*Five billion years ago*
Where	*The Universe*
Why	*Heaven*
How	*Gas, dust, and rock*
Action	*Stars and sunlight*
Circumstance	*Satan, the Morning Star*
Dominion	*Lucifer*
Special	*Adam*
Time	*The beginning of civilization*

Introduction

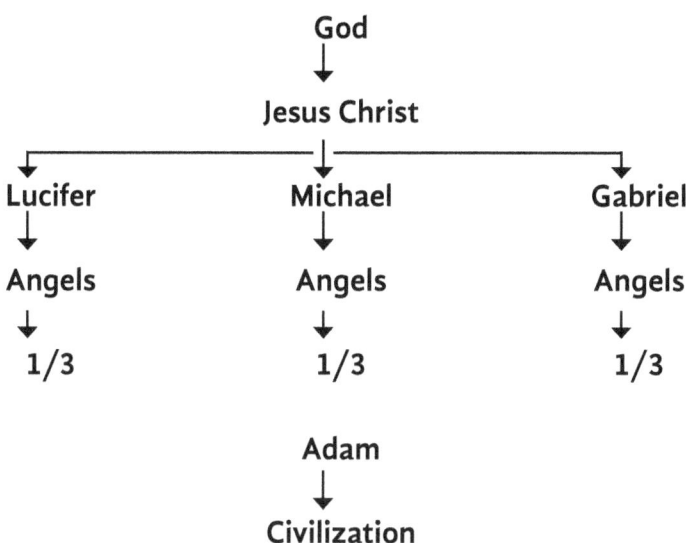

God says:

"People worshiped the dragon because he had given authority to the beast..." (Revelation 13:4).

THE BEAST HAS POWER TO DESTROY, but that power comes from a dragon that is being worshipped! A false church, the Pope who dominates the Roman Catholic Church. They worshipped the beast, the devil. People are worshipping a war machine.

WHAT IS EARTH?

EARTH IS ONE OF EIGHT PLANETS that continually circle the sun making up the Solar System. It is the third planet out from the sun. Between Venus and Mars, and like them and Mercury, the planet nearest to the sun. Earth is a ball made largely of rock. What makes it special is the fact that its' surface is covered by two-thirds water. It is also the only planet with oxygen in its atmosphere. Without water and oxygen there would be no life.

No one is absolutely sure of how earth was formed or how it began, but most astronomers think that about five billion years ago there was just a vast cloud of hot gas and dust circling around the newly-formed sun. Then, gradually, part of this cloud began to clump together, pulled together by gravity. This clump grew to form the planets.

The earth turns around within a 24 hour period, this is why days are 24 hours long. But because earth moves around the sun while turning, it takes exactly 24 hours to return to the same place in the sky.

The earth is 93 million miles from the sun on average but it varies according to the time of the year. Its closest distance is on January 3. This is how far the earth is from the sun. We get seasons because earth is always tilted over in the same direction. So when earth is on one side of the sun, the Northern Hemisphere is tilted toward the sun, bringing summer here. When earth is on the other side of the sun, the Northern Hemisphere is tilted away, bringing winter. The seasons are reversed in the South.

In earlier times, people thought the earth was at the center of the universe. They were so sure of their ideas that they became very angry with scientists who said they were wrong. Today we are still learning about the earth, the moon, the sun, and the strange and beautiful things our universe contains. This we know for sure: our world is just one of many specks in space, and not the center of things at all, but it's our home.

People also used to think that the sun rotated around the earth. It's easy to see why people thought so. When we get up very early in the morning, we see the sun appear down low in the sky and throughout the day it seems to travel across the sky until it sets or disappears, just before night. This movement of the sun gave people the idea that the sun was circling the earth, but they had things backward. It is the earth that spins or rotates like a top. The sun doesn't really rise or set at all. It is the spinning of the earth that makes it look that way. It's easy to understand when we look straight ahead and the earth spins around very fast. Things seem to move around about us in a circle, but really we are the ones doing the moving.

GENESIS

"In the beginning God created the heavens and the earth. Now the earth was formless and empty, darkness was over the surface of the deep, and the Spirit of God was hovering over the waters. And God said, 'Let there be light,' and there was light. God saw that the light was good, and he separated the light from the darkness. God called the light 'day,' and the darkness he called 'night.' And there was evening, and there was morning—the first day. And God said, 'Let there be a vault between the waters to separate water from water.' So God made the vault and separated the water under the vault from the water above it. And it was so. God called the vault 'sky.' And there was evening, and there was morning—the second day." (Genesis 1:1-8).

ALL THIS WAS CREATED BY GOD billions of years ago. He created everything, and the solar system, in a six-epoch time period, six moments, or six days, as man prefers and would like to interpret.

So God made the earth, the universe, the stars and the solar system, the sun and all of heaven. The question is, who is this God? He created all of this firmament, for what purpose? What was His intention, and where was all this leading to five millions years ago? Five million years ago God must have had millions of angels in heaven. God created man almost 7,000 years ago, a human being which is too far for us to comprehend (Genesis 2:7). A phenomena as large as this, and in our little time, some of us human beings try to understand, and yet those who understand keep mute. We do have a Holy Bible given to us by God, and it tell us about the truth, the whole truth and nothing but the truth. But the Book of Revelation is more than just truth. Reality still is the obscurity. God is the truth, and what's more, He loves us and looks after us every which way.

The question among ourselves is, why were we human beings put on this earth? If we read and study the Bible constantly, and seek not only the truth but reality, we will be surprised and amazed at the strong emotional reaction and marvelous attention. Some of us will not agree with the simple reason because we human beings don't believe what we don't see. To get to the point, are we human beings here on this earth by coincidence or existence? This simply means, we human beings were not meant to be here or anywhere. Why? Because humans are just a simple substitute to serve as a replacement usually for a time, and it is getting shorter every day. The 7,000 years since man was made is just about over. The Third World War is just around the corner. For our ignorance, stupidity and disobedience to God we are going to burn (Matthew 24:15-25). One push of a button and this earth will be in flames. We human beings are here just by circumstance. God created us in His own image (Genesis 2:5-7) to replace who? Lucifer and his army of evil angels. One-third of evil angels led by Satan, the supreme personification of evil ruler of hell, which today is known as the devil, Lucifer, the most attractive beauteous, gorgeous and handsome angel God created. He is called the Morning Star on this earth.

ADAM

> "Then God said, 'Let us make mankind in our image, in our likeness, so that they may rule over the fish in the sea and the birds in the sky, over the livestock and all the wild animals,[a] and over all the creatures that move along the ground.'"
> (Genesis 1:26).

GOD CREATED HIM MALE AND FEMALE and to be fruitful and multiply. Human beings are not created like angels. Adam and Eve are our first parents. Because of Eve, when we are born, we have an umbilical cord and a navel. Angels don't.

> "Then the Lord God formed a man from the dust of the ground and breathed into his nostrils the breath of life, and the man became a living being." (Genesis 2:7).

Lucifer became rebellious and disobedient against God. *"And there was war in heaven..."* (Isaiah 14:12; Revelation 12:7-9). Lucifer, Satan, was cast out of heaven. Him, the devil, and one-third of his evil angels, they all chose and settled on planet earth millions of years ago. All of this happened before Adam came to be. But for his contravene with God, Lucifer and all his one-third of evil angels, continued to willfully ignore God's commandment to finish the earth project. This resulted in the earth being without form, void and unattended, and darkness was on the face of the deep. God had to intervene to modify and settle things out with action, and with the help of archangels Michael and Gabriel, God finished planet earth, thus heaven and all the host of the universe were finished on the sixth day or moment. And God rested on the seventh day, a five billion year period. God needed an attendant here on earth. Therefore, God created Adam, and later Eve, in the most perfect form. So well made that not even today's medical scientists or any specialists in science or biology have yet discovered another perfect human being, like Adam and Eve.

In a way, Adam was like any of God's angels. God placed him in the Garden of Eden (Genesis 2:15), the most beautiful place on earth, a land of paradise. Adam was to attend and administer all living things and issues on earth. In those days man was of high stature on the gigantic scale, and could live to 500 years or more. Adam lived to be 930 years and passed on.

God caused a deep sleep to fall on Adam and he slept. Remember, Adam is God's statesman, representative of the world's affairs. He never slept and was always awake, like God and the angels. So while Adam slept God took one of Adam's rib and made with it a woman, then brought her to the man. Adam called her Eve and she became his wife.

In a way, Adam replaced Lucifer and all his evil angels here on earth. Remember, Satan was cast out from heaven. He and all of his evil angels chose the planet earth to be his headquarters. Satan became jealous and angry at God and from that moment on seeks revenge against God. He believed that by destroying Adam, or mankind in this world he could hurt God, and God's plan on earth.

FALL OF MAN

LUCIFER, OR SATAN, being crafty, tempted and deceived Eve, persuading her and Adam, her husband, to commit sin against God. The devil convinced them to do and believe lying, false statements about God. The serpent told them they could be like God and be forever like Him. When God found out what Adam and Eve had done, He became very angry at them. Adam and Eve were both cast out of the Garden of Eden to till the ground from which Adam was taken, and drove them out on their own. Adam would no longer have eternal life, would eventually die, and rest as a reward to him. Because of that sin all his children and their children, and all mankind will know death as a reward for all generations to come.

Adam had sexual intercourse with his wife Eve and conceived Cain, and shortly thereafter Abel. Cain was a farmer and Abel a shepherd, he took care of his flock. Cain was always jealous of his younger brother. Abel was always obedient and closer to God. One day while out in the field, Cain out of anger and jealousy killed, murdered his brother Abel, and blood and hatred entered the world, still is and is worse today. An infamy stain is on man's hands. God put a curse on Cain. God didn't kill Cain for the same reason God didn't kill the devil, but God did set a mark on Cain and banished him from the land to be a fugitive, a drifter, a tramp, and a vagabond. To this day, he is still wandering the earth from place to place.

The punishment was too much for Cain to bear. He was afraid and feared being killed himself. Cain pleaded with God for mercy and countenance. God said,

> "But the Lord said to him, 'Not so; anyone who kills Cain will suffer vengeance seven times over.' Then the Lord put a mark on Cain so that no one who found him would kill him."
> (Genesis 4:15).

So God put a mark on Cain as a warning to others. For whosoever fights or does battle with Cain, his mark will show his valor and superiority among his hostiles. His Anglo-Saxon, white mark will distinguish him from all races in the world. Beginning with Cain to the American colonies, anyone who rises up against them will perish, seven times seven they will perish.

Adam and Eve had many more children. Eve became the mother of all the living. Today, there are nearly eight billion people in the world (2019). The devil has tempted all humans and each one of them to slaughter one another in all kinds of world wars. But the devil has not triumphed because God still remembers Adam and Cain. Yes! We human beings are ignorant, inexperienced and maybe fools, but we are not stupid. We still believe in God, one God and still remember His Ten Commandments and His Sabbath, and God loves us. The hell with Satan.

HUMANS SUCCEED FALLEN ANGELS

GOD THEN PROPOSED to reproduce himself through humans made in His image and likeness, but made from internal flesh, bone, and blood, and subject to death if there is sin. Humans and angels are not made the same, but there is no disrespect for one or the other. Humans are begotten by God, and that is what caused God to do this most colossal, tremendous thing ever. God's supreme, overall purpose is to create, even to this extent of reproducing himself, and also reign supreme over all His creation. Apparently, God has chosen this earth to become His universe headquarters and seat of the supreme throne of God.

Now, God proposed to restore His government over the years through man, created in His image, and finally to become part of God's family. The good news is God's purpose for mankind, and the fact that the two-thirds of the angels who are holy and righteous outnumber the demons, and remain as God's invisible agents to minister and help in the righteous character development of the myriad of humans who shall yet become the sons and heirs of the supreme God, members of the great God family. That is why God put man on earth.

> "Then the Lord God formed a man from the dust of the ground and breathed into his nostrils the breath of life, and the man became a living being." (Genesis 2:7).

He was named Adam and was placed in the Garden of Eden to administer and supervise all of God the Father's affairs as full commander-in-chief with no limitations and, like God, he never rested or slept.

What then is man? He is a living being made from the dust of the ground. Man is clay and God is the master potter, molding, shaping, and forming our character if we respond when He calls and draws us to Him. God created man on the earth to build in us what the sinning angels refused to let God build in them —His perfect character! He is in His time-order and way developing us to become very God, each of us, and to finish the creation of the unfinished universe.

For now, we still live in this deceived world led by Satan.

THE GREAT FLOOD

SO ADAM LIVED up to 930 years and passed on, and the world began to fulfill God's command to multiply and to replenish the earth (Genesis 9:1). Man became so numerous and without a true sense of direction. He began to live much his own way wild, disorderly and desperate. Through time, these conducts began to show in the most hypocritical, pitiful, and virulent manner.

God saw that the weakness of man was great on the earth, and that every intent of the thoughts of man's heart was only evil continually.

> "The Lord regretted that he had made human beings on the earth, and his heart was deeply troubled. 'So the Lord said, "I will wipe from the face of the earth the human race I have created—and with them the animals, the birds and the creatures that move along the ground—for I regret that I have made them.'"
> (Genesis 6:6-7).

But Noah found grace in the eyes of the Lord. Noah was a just man, perfect in his generation. Noah walked with God, and God spoke with Noah, telling him,

> "So make yourself an ark of cypress wood; make rooms in it and coat it with pitch inside and out." (Genesis 6:14).

> "You are to bring into the ark two of all living creatures, male and female, to keep them alive with you." (Genesis 6:19).

> "You are to take every kind of food that is to be eaten and store it away as food for you and for them." (Genesis 6:21).

Noah did according to all that God commanded him.

It took Noah and his three sons Shem, Ham and Japheth 120 years to complete the ark. After completion, Noah, his three sons and their wives together, with all living flesh animals, two by two, entered the ark and the big door was shut. Then the Lord let it rain on the earth 40 days and 40 nights, and then the rain stopped. The water remained for about 12 more weeks.

The earth was covered with water. Nothing remained alive. Noah waited another three months for the water to subside. When dry land appeared, everyone in the ark disembarked. They walked out onto dry land to roam the land. The ark rested on top of Mount Ararat, 16,854 feet high, in the northern part of Turkey. The flood destroyed every living being on the earth, and all living things perished. Noah built an altar, made sacrifices and gave thanks to the Lord, and he also gave an offering of a young lamb to God. God was pleased with Noah. It was a new beginning; God then commanded them to,

> "...be fruitful and increase in number; multiply on the earth and increase upon it." (Genesis 9:7).

Now, the sons of Noah who went out of the Ark were Shem, Ham, and Japheth. Ham was the father of Canaan (he is also considered the father of all Black people today). From the sons of Noah, the whole earth was repopulated. These were the families of the sons of Noah according to their generations. From their nations and from these nations they were divided on earth after the flood.

> **"Noah lived a total of 950 years, and then he died."**
> **(Genesis 9:29).**

SHEM GERMAN'S ROOT

HUNDREDS OF YEARS AFTER the flood were perhaps the most crucial in human history. The inhabitant descendants of Noah began to spread out to green valleys, from the mountains of Ararat to the plains in the land of Shinar (Mesopotamia), and along the Tigris and Euphrates rivers, a rich, fertilized land for agriculture, and down to the Persian Gulf. Genesis 10 gives a brief account of this occurrence, mainly listing the lineages of Noah's three sons Ham, Shem and Japheth, all of them of dark complexion. (Shem was fair-skinned and had lighter hair.) They developed their own ideas, became overpopulated, did not obey God, and started worshiping idols.

God drew special attention to Nimrod, son of Cush, grandson of Ham, and great-grandson of Noah. Nimrod means to rebel against God. He became a tyrant and organized competitions. He built the Tower of Babel, the original Babylon, and ancient Nineveh (Jonah 1:2).

Nimrod founded the Babylonian system that has gripped the world ever since. Nimrod was so evil, it is said he married his own mother, whose name was Semiramis, a woman who became known as the Babylonian "Queen of Heaven." While Nimrod was alive, he had put himself in the place of God by dictatorial rule. His admirers called him "Baal." After Nimrod's death, Semiramis became ruler of her son's kingdom, and she was used by Satan to spread an evil doctrine. She was worshiped as the queen of heaven. She also committed fornication with the leading men of that time. Traditions suggest that Nimrod may have been executed by Shem, son of Noah, who deeply opposed Nimrod's rebellion against God. Shem walked mostly in the ways of God.

Genesis 10:22 indicates that Shem, the third son of Noah, had five children: Elam, Asshur, Arphaxad, Lud, and Aram. Asshur was the son of Shem and the father of the White strain lineage (Cain), and those of fair skin and lighter hair. These are the generations of Shem (Genesis 11:10). Neither of Shem's first two sons Elam and Asshur are mentioned because they were rejected as heirs of Shem's inheritance. They were close and worked alongside of Nimrod, so we can see why Shem rejected them.

We should note that in Genesis 9:20-25, after the flood,

> "Noah, a man of the soil, proceeded to plant a vineyard. When he drank some of its wine, he became drunk and lay uncovered inside his tent. Ham, the father of Canaan, saw his father naked and told his two brothers outside. But Shem and Japheth took a garment and laid it across their shoulders; then they walked in backward and covered their father's naked body. Their faces were turned the other way so that they would not see their father naked. When Noah awoke from his wine and found out what his youngest son had done to him, he said, 'Cursed be Canaan! The lowest of slaves will he be to his brothers.'"

A Black slave. Ham is the father of all the Black people.

After Elam and Asshur were rejected as heirs of Shem's inheritance, and because they worked along with Nimrod, Asshur parted away from his father and became the progenitor of the Assyrian people. Ancient Assyrians acquired a new and different language. In the days of Nimrod, he constructed the Tower of Babel, capital city of a world-ruling dictatorship. To bring this project to a halt, God had to intervene to keep civilization from progressing to a point of self-destruction, God confounded their language (Genesis 11:7). They moved about and distributed themselves over an area along the Euphrates and Tigris rivers, by Syria and Iraq, in modern-day Western Asia. That's when most of the Syrians acquired the Indo-Germanic tongue, which was akin to Old High German, the language of the people who inhabited Assyria, which was not merrily Semitic. Elam, grandson of Noah and the son of Shem, and Nimrod, great-grandson of Noah, rebelled against God. Nimrod established the kingdom of Babylon.

It is significant that Asshur, the father of the Assyrians, and Arphaxad, whose line Abraham descended from, both came from Shem. There were physical differences between the Assyrian and the Israelites; both people came from the fair-skinned, White racial strain of Shem (the mark of Cain). Considering the early beginning of the Assyrian people, and concerning Asshur, son of Shem, who had five sons. Asshur lived in the city of Nineveh, and named his subjects Assyrians, who became the most fortunate nation beyond others. Assyria quickly became the most prosperous and powerful nation of the day. Later, much later, the line of Asshur unfolded apart to extend in time to Europe, bordering on the Arctic (North Ocean), the Atlantic Ocean (West), the Mediterranean Sea (South), and the Ural Mountains. With him, the Indo-Germanic tongue and numerous words of which were akin to Old High German. All of the fair-skinned White racial strain of Shem and all of the lighter hair, which make us think about the "Mark of Cain," a vagabond, a wandering Anglo-Saxon, a member of the German people. Cain settled in the Scandinavian country in the time of Adam, where North Germanic languages were spoken. Much later they were known as the Vikings in the 8th century, an English vagabond, all in all becoming the greatest warriors the world has ever known.

This also makes us think that Asshur settled in Assyria, in the Middle East. His children could very well have settled in Europe, becoming German-Dutch and English White Anglo-Saxon, a very prosperous people and hard to kill. It has been proved in our late 19th century, and in two World Wars. But in the 20th century, Germany was still the strongest country in the world, and it will be involved in the next Third World War, soon to explode. God help us. The German are great people, but they have a long history with the Holy Roman Empire. This empire has a history of bloodshed like no other institution in at least 2000 years. The Bible prophecies Germany and other nations will make up the coming Holy Roman Empire and 10 kings.

The Germans (Shem's son Elam and Asshur) are behaving the way the Holy Roman Empire has always behaved. Germany is once again seeking to impose its will on the world. The Bible prophecies that this Holy Roman Empire would rise repeatedly in Europe. In World War II, Adolf Hitler led the sixth resurrection of this power, which caused the death of approximately 60 million people. Germany also started World War I, which cost 15 to 19 million lives, approximately. The crown of the Holy Roman Empire. Hitler called his Nazi empire the Third Reich, after the first Germanic Reich of the Second Reich of the German Empire.

The Germans rule more than just Germany. Today, they want to control the internet, and that is only a step away from controlling the world. Germany's ambitions for the internet should concern everyone, even those who don't own a computer.

In Daniel 8:25, a Third World War is described. Germany and the Holy Roman Empire will stand up against the Prince of Peace, and the false lamb, but will be broken but without human hand. The Book of Revelation 17:13 tells us the same thing, describing the coming of these 10 kings. These have one mind and give their power and strength into "The Beast." Verse 14 says those shall make war with the true "Lamb." These nations and 10 kings are also going to make war with Jesus Christ himself.

> "They will wage war against the Lamb, but the Lamb will triumph over them because he is Lord of lords and King of kings—and with him will be his called, chosen and faithful followers." (Revelations 17:14).

And how will it end? The Lamb shall overcome them. He is the Lord, King of kings, and those with Him are called, chosen and faithful.

The Holy Roman Empire's power is about to be destroyed forever. Remember, we are living in our last days since Adam. So today, those who had the opportunity, who are called and chosen, will be at Jesus Christ's side when He returns the second time.

WHO ARE WE?

WHY DOES MAN have thinking and reasoning and possesses all human funds of knowledge, which is impossible for animals to have? Is he an immortal soul, and if so, why? Better yet, why is mankind here on earth? Did he simply happen? Or, was there a design and purpose for him? Of course, we say there is a cause and effect; the effect is we are here.

Higher education does not know the answers to these questions, and doesn't want to know. Man is more interested in war, and history has proved it in many ways. When we raise the question of what and why, the intellectuals and people of knowledge just simply shy away or stand up and fight off the question of what and why is man, and willingly ignore it. So secular education shuts its mind and its mouth in tight silence.

Science doesn't know the answer. Religion does not reveal it either because it also doesn't know. Incredible, but true. Why is this willful ignorance? Because God is involved. Satan is hostile against God. Satan is on the throne of this earth, and has blinded the minds of the intellectuals as well as educated people and all other levels of society. Their ignorance cannot be explained except by the invisible and unaware influence of the supernatural evil power of Satan, the devil, and the unseen demonical spirit beings. The world has been deceived by Satan. Jesus Christ, thank God that the truth is hidden from the wise and prudent, and revealed to those who are babes in materialistic knowledge. Instead of improving, beautifying, and completing earth's creation, the sinning angels brought earth, and mankind, to desolation and ruin in every which way.

In Genesis 1:2, the Bible says:

> **"Now the earth was formless and empty, darkness was over the surface of the deep, and the Spirit of God was hovering over the waters."**

"Without form" and "void" means wasted, desolated, and deteriorated. The word "was" is also translated as became. So possibly, after five billion years, all had come to be oceanic surface and light had been turned into darkness by angelic lawlessness, which also means that God, before the creation of this earth and universe, must have had hundreds of thousands of angelic beings, if not millions, some good and some bad, starting with Lucifer, later called Satan, and much later the devil. Bear in mind, this is millions of years ago, even before Adam and Eve came to be.

We need to notice here that Lucifer, the Morning Star, as he is known today, allotted himself and tried once or twice to seize God's throne in heaven. "And there was war in heaven." (Isaiah 14:12-13 and Revelation 12:7-9). Remember, God created Lucifer. He made him tall, beautiful, handsome and intelligent, and put him in charge of the new earth to come five billion years ago. But while the earth was still without form and in darkness, Lucifer went bad and became jealous, and his band of evil angels, one-third of all the angels, separated from God. God threw him and all his one-third of evil angels out and away from heaven. And Lucifer founded a home on an earth that was still without form, void and wasted for many more millions of years, until God made light and day and finished and completed earth. And the earth flourished many billions of years later.

After the earth was made complete and finished, Adam was created by God to be His attendant here on earth and to be in charge of all living things. But not as an angel, not as an animal, but as a human being perfect and handsome.

THE MORNING STAR

THE ARCHANGEL LUCIFER was just one of two covering cherubs created by God. A perfect angel created by God. But Lucifer became arrogant and evil. He is also known as Satan or the devil. Satan's primary goal is to destroy God's work and His people. The devil has tremendous power in this world. This is a reality in the history of the church and in this world.

> "The god of this age has blinded the minds of unbelievers, so that they cannot see the light of the gospel that displays the glory of Christ, who is the image of God."
> (2 Corinthians 4:4).

So he has deceived mankind into believing he doesn't even exist! This is Satan's world, and he is the invisible god of this world, author of its organization, basic philosophies, its systems of government, business, society, and yes, religions too, like the Catholic religion and the Pope.

Satan moves in the human spirit, within people, to move them in attitudes of envy, jealousy, resentment, impatience, bitterness and strife. For more than five billion years since God began to build the universe, Lucifer has envied God, and has carried deep strife and

My God We Will Perish

jealousy toward God, to even want to destroy God! Satan was thrown out of heaven (Isaiah 14:12) because he wanted to be like the Most High God. God will put an end to Satan in due time in our resurrection period.

THE BEGINNING OF CIVILIZATION

SATAN IS CALLED the "prince of the power of the air," and he is working inside the minds of people. At the beginning of Adam, God designed a 7,000 year master plan for accomplishing His tremendous purpose. In the first 1,000 years we see Adam doing his upmost things for humanity. Like Cain, Abel and Noah. Adam lived to be 930 years old, and nearly 2,000 years the human lifespan from Adam to Noah averaged another 900 years. So think about it. The first man, Adam, lived nearly one-sixth of all the time human creation until now has lived at our present world timetable (2019), which is 7,000 years since Adam.

This clearly means we are living in the last days. And what have we to show? Disobedience to God and God's law, which defines all the evils, sorrows, pain and suffering years of human civilization that has resulted in 7,000 years. The first 6,000 years were allotted to allow Satan to remain on earth's throne, and for humanity to learn the bitter lesson. Remember, Adam's 930 years plus 6,000 years allotted to Satan and for humanity to learn our bitter lesson through experience, equals the 7,000 year span. Also, we need to remember the world had never known of the existence of God the Father until Jesus Christ came and revealed the Father (Matthew 11:27). The world, from its foundation,

My God We Will Perish

was cut off from God the Father. Jesus came to reconcile repentant believers to the Father (Romans 5:10).

The point here is we, humanity, are living on the planet, our world, in our last days, and what have we to show for it. Corruption, violence, crime, injustice, sickness, broken homes, destruction, World War I, World War II, and perhaps World War III is just around the corner.

God, have mercy on us.

TRUTH IS FALLEN

IN TODAY'S MEDIA-BASED WORLD, both mainstream and alternative news, sources have moved away from objectively reporting the truth in favor of more biased, opinion-based messages. Truth simply isn't valued as it once was.

The only hope of justice, peace, truth and right solutions to all the world's problems is the coming in power and glory of Jesus Christ to set up a world government. Right government. The government of God!

Light will replace darkness. Truth will replace error. Understanding will replace crass materialism. True knowledge will replace intellectual ignorance. The truth is precious beyond words. We can be filled with hope knowing that it will soon saturate all media.

The Bible given to us by God foretold a time when media and society would not value the truth.

> "No one calls for justice; no one pleads a case with integrity. They rely on empty arguments, they utter lies; they conceive trouble and give birth to evil."…"So justice is driven back, and righteousness stands at a distance; truth has stumbled in the streets, honesty cannot enter. Truth is nowhere to be found, and whoever shuns evil becomes a prey. The Lord looked and was displeased that there was no justice." (Isaiah 59:4; 14-15).

NUCLEAR ARSENAL

EXPERTS TELL US that once a nuclear war starts, it cannot be stopped. Such a monstrous nuclear power like the one possessed by Russia, Iran, China and North Korea impacts this world. The nuclear "genie" is out of the bottle. We have reached the point of no return. How can these words and events not strike fear in all of us? The earth is like a ticking nuclear bomb waiting to explode. The world is so corruptive it takes only a mad politician to push a button, to turn a small knob, and the world is set on fire. Our earth will be no more.

The world is in a kind of madness state. It is precisely how Jesus Christ prophesied almost 2,000 years ago. It would be the end of time.

> **"For then there will be great distress, unequaled from the beginning of the world until now—and never to be equaled again. If those days had not been cut short, no one would survive, but for the sake of the elect those days will be shortened."**
> **(Matthew 24:21-22).**

Not one person or animal would be alive!

Does this media-based world carry more weight with us than Christ's own words? Do we listen to our political leaders more than we need to listen to Christ's own warning? It's time for plain speaking, repentance, forgiving, seeking, praying and writing.

My God We Will Perish

All we need to do is understand the Bible, which tell us to watch the world's events. Bible prophecy says this will indeed happen. World War III is just around the corner. God help us.

THE TWO-HORNED BEAST

IT ALL STARTED on a stark rocky island called Patmos, in Greece, by the Mediterranean Sea in Europe. That is where John the Apostle wrote the terrible prophecies that became the Book of Revelation. Jesus Christ's youngest apostle, now at 95 years old, was being held prisoner at Patmos. John, the revelator, rapt in vision, wrote what he saw...fantastic strange beasts, clashing armies, nations rising.

> "The dragon stood on the shore of the sea. And I saw a beast coming out of the sea. It had ten horns and seven heads, with ten crowns on its horns, and on each head a blasphemous name. The beast I saw resembled a leopard, but had feet like those of a bear and a mouth like that of a lion. The dragon gave the beast his power and his throne and great authority."
> (Revelation 13:1-2.)

The Pope. We need to note that water-sea stands for people; seven heads and ten horns stand for kings and European countries or kingdoms in Europe, all worshiping a false church; the Catholic Pope stands for the image of the Beast; horns represent kings or rulers.

In Revelation 13:11-13, John adds:

> "Then I saw a second beast, coming out of the earth. It had two horns like a lamb, but it spoke like a dragon. It exercised all the

> authority of the first beast on its behalf, and made the earth and its inhabitants worship the first beast, whose fatal wound had been healed. And it performed great signs, even causing fire to come down from heaven to the earth in full view of the people."

In prophecy, beast represents a kingdom (Daniel 7:23). When a beast comes "out of the sea," (Revelation 13:1) it represents many people and multitudes. When a beast comes "out of the earth," it means the opposite, so here is a nation springing up out of the wilderness area. Instead of overthrowing other power to establish itself, this nation would rise in territory previously unoccupied. It would be a country that is discovered, differing from the often blood-soaked nations of Europe. This nation would spring up quietly, peacefully "like a lamb." We guess right: a new nation arose into power, giving promise of strength and greatness. This description fits the United States of America. The U.S. sprung out like a plant from the ground, "like a silent seed that grows into an empire."

"It had two horns like a lamb" (Revelation 13:11), indicates youth, gentleness, and it also represents civil and religious freedom, but the beast with the lamb-like horns "spoke like a dragon," like a false lamb (Protestant), and exercised all the power of the first beast, the Catholic Pope before him, and dwells there in to worship the beast and kept Sunday like Catholicism (Revelation 11:13). Incredible! Get ready for a shock!

The following mind-boggling statements were made by Catholic Church authorities, and are documented.

Question: Do you have any other way of proving that the Church (Roman Catholic) has power to institute festival precepts?

Answer: The Catholic Church has no such power. She could not have done that in which all modern religions agree with her. She could not have substituted the observance of Sunday, the first day of the week, for the observance of Saturday, the seventh day, a change for which there is no scriptural authority. Incredible! The Catholic Church of her divine mission changed the day from Saturday to Sunday.

Question: Which is the Sabbath Day?

Answer: Saturday is the Sabbath Day.

Question: Why do we observe Sunday instead of Saturday?

Answer: We observe Sunday instead of Saturday because the Catholic Church, in the Council of Laodicea, transferred the solemnity from Saturday to Sunday.

The Fourth Commandment actually says:

> "Remember the Sabbath day by keeping it holy. Six days you shall labor and do all your work, but the seventh day is a Sabbath to the LORD your God, on which you must not do any work—neither you, nor your son or daughter, nor your manservant or maidservant or livestock, nor the foreigner within your gates. For in six days the LORD made the heavens and the earth and the sea and all that is in them, but on the seventh day He rested. Therefore the LORD blessed the Sabbath day and set it apart as holy." (Exodus 20: 8-11).

Jesus said,

> "They worship me in vain; their teachings are merely human rules." (Matthew 15:9).

This is why God tells it like it is, because He is love. Remember, there are many sincere people, lovely Christians in this fallen church, and they will hear God's call, and will come out.

Here is a list of symbols and what they represent:

The Beast: Satan, the devil

The image of the beast: The Pope (second beast)

The mark of the beast: Catholicism

The false lamb: Protestants in the USA (Rev. 13:11-13)

Finally, both Catholics and Protestants observe and keep Sunday, and worship the beast. God help us in resurrection time.

A DELIVERER

> "Then God said, 'Let us make mankind in our image, in our likeness, so that they may rule over the fish in the sea and the birds in the sky, over the livestock and all the wild animals, and over all the creatures that move along the ground.'"
> (Genesis 1:26).

WHO IS GOD TALKING TO when He said "Let us make?" Who is "us?" Obviously it has to be the Holy Trinity. The word trinity is something made from us. But according to the Book of Revelation, God is using plural form. It leaves a gap open for questions, doesn't it?

In the first book of the Bible, the Book of Genesis, God ended His work in both heaven and earth, a creation of six days, and He rested on the seventh day. Archaeologically speaking, we know it means the earth was made in six days. A period of something. A period of time in terms of worthy events. Moments of times conducted in millions of years or better of each day as it is. When it came to the sixth day or period of time, God made man and woman in His image. As for the seventh day, He rested. We know God never rests or ever rested.

My God We Will Perish

Neither does Satan. Neither God nor Satan have an umbilical cord, a navel like we do. So Satan never rests, he doesn't need to. However, the seventh day is applicable for us, and so the seventh day is made for us to rest and worship based on a 24-hour day as it is our time of day. It was never or ever in reference to God while making earth and the universe.

Biologists or historians haven't come out with any of these theories. So we don't know what God really looks like because there is not really an answer. God is and always was and always will be infinite. No one has seen God and lived to tell about it. God has made appearances in some forms, yes, and still is. In the Old Testament to Adam and later Cain, God did speak to them, later to Noah, and much later to Job and Abraham. Then on to Moses (Exodus 3:2). God spoke to Moses face to face in form of fire.

Did Moses see God? Did Moses see an image of human form or being? Of course not! Out there in the wilderness, the only thing Moses saw was a bright burning bush. That is the only time and close examination that we know to its existence that any human like us even came close to seeing God. Moses wrote the first five books of the Old Testament, six if you include the book of Job. All are attributed to Moses.

I might add here that before Moses, we had Abraham, from the land of Ur (Iran today). Three men appeared to Abraham in human form (Genesis 18:1-10). While in the land of Canaan, all three men looking alike; we know they were the Holy Trinity. God the Father, God the Son, and God the Holy Spirit. All three had similar appearances. This is what Abraham saw and spoke with in human form.

They appeared to Abraham to discuss the coming of the birth of a child, as well to inherit the earth and from his seed to multiply and be as many as the stars in heaven and the sand of the sea, and be God's

A Deliverer

chosen people. A selected people from this new birth child yet to be born and bring salvation to the world, a great nation. The child's name was Isaac.

Coming back to Moses, God spoke to Him not by appearance but by voice, the voice of God for a good purpose, to lead His chosen people and educate them to be a special people to bring good examples to the rest of the world, and to believe only in one God. He also gave them His Ten Commandments, and Jesus also told us that we need to be born again in heart and spirit. And 3,000 years later in baptism.

It's hard and complicated for the Jewish people, the children of God, to accept and believe the true word of salvation and obedience. In His plan of salvation, God chose Moses to establish and direct His people. In time and much further in life God's people, the Jewish, began to rebel and become imprudent and prominent so a deliverer was necessary to come to the world to renovate the law of God.

A savior is born from the line of Rahab —a harlot—, and the Virgin Mary (Joshua 6:25), from David the king to Jesus Christ, full of grace, the Messiah. With the assistance of Paul, His servant, did the same as Moses did. And the Old Testament is renovated into a New Testament.

What a wonderful God we have!

WORLD CRISIS AT THE END

THE 7,000 YEAR PERIOD after Adam's sin is now at its end. Today, man's world is reeling on its last legs. War, violence, destruction and terrorism engulfs the entire world. Half the world exists in ignorance and poverty, frustrated with crime, alcoholism and drug abuse. Mankind is nearing the end of its rope, as in the days of Noah. At last the weapons of mass destruction have been invented, are produced and possessed by many nations, and they can erase all life on planet earth. In these last days of mankind's last gasping for air, Jesus Christ foretold how it would end.

> "And this gospel of the kingdom will be preached in the whole world as a testimony to all nations, and then the end will come." (Matthew 24:14).

This Gospel now has been preached into every nation. For the first time in history, nuclear energy has developed with the capacity to destroy every human alive on earth. Jesus foretold the Great Tribulation, a time of trouble so great that unless God does intervene, no human being will be saved alive. For the sake of His Church, God will intervene supernaturally before the total destruction of humanity (Matthew 24:31-41). These are the very last days for Satan.

My God We Will Perish

The world's number one concern today is the question of survival! Science and technology have dropped the weapons of mass destruction that could blast all human life on this earth! Some nations possess nuclear weapons that all it takes is another Nimrod, another Hitler or evil madman to ignite the nuclear World War III, which could obliterate all human life from this planet. Yet, the truth of God, which is known and acted on, could save humanity from this threat and all its evils.

We live in a world seemingly far advanced in science, technology, higher education and diffusion of knowledge. People think it's a world of great progress. We sent men to the Moon and returned them safely back to earth. Unmanned spacecraft land on Mars, fly close to Jupiter and send back astonishing pictures of Jupiter and the rings of Saturn. Surgeons transplant human hearts and other human organs. It's a push-button world of things where work is done largely by machines.

The internet, computers and cell phones are at its highest. What can we say? It's all in its greatest virtue and greatest evil. Perpetrator yet of its tool of the worst of men, perhaps the product of so many men in its purest production, and surest thing men have in this world in use.

Sometimes we need to be reminded of how horrible man can be toward his fellowmen. There is probably no greater example of inhumanity than the disastrous World War II. How much of it have we forgotten? Have we completely shut it out of our mind? Do we think it won't happen again? God said it's going to happen far worse than ever before. God help us.

THE SECOND ADAM

IN THE BEGINNING, since the creation of Adam, a timetable of 7,000 year period was set. Soon after, Adam became weak and disobedient to God. He no longer would be like God. His penalty would be death as a reward for him and all his generations to come. Today we are near the end of that timetable. A new Adam is needed. Two thousand years ago, a Savior came to this world to show us the way to salvation, and to know God the Father. His name is Jesus Christ, a Messiah as the Second Adam, the reason the wily and evil Satan had been invisibly swaging and ruling mankind cut-off from all contact with and knowledge of God.

Satan still sits at the throne of power in the world, though not administering God's government, but subtlety swaging all humanity to live under the precise opposite to the law of God's government, to the way of vanity, bitterness and sorrow, courting, competition, strife and violence, instead of living in God's way of outflowing love, peace, happiness and joy.

Jesus did not come to save Satan's world while the devil sits on the world's throne, deceiving humanity. Jesus will save the world in His Second Coming, when Satan will be put away. Why, then, did Jesus come more than 2,000 years ago? He came not to rule, not to reign over nations, not to save the world while Satan still rules over it. Jesus' human birth was the arrival of the "Second Adam." He came to qualify where the First Adam *failed*, and to replace the former Archangel Lucifer on earth's throne, and to rule with the government of God. Jesus came to announce the future establishment of the Kingdom of God, to teach the prophetic Good News (the Gospel) to His chosen future apostles. He came to make Himself our direct creator. The penalty for our sin was His death on the cross so that we might share the Good News to the world. Jesus had come to die and to be resurrected from the dead by God, making His Second Coming for all who are willing to receive Him as Savior of all humanity, who have ever lived on this earth. And He came to establish God's Church to train the believers to rule under Him.

THE LOVE OF GOD

THE LOVE OF GOD is greater far
Than tongue or pen can ever tell
It goes beyond the highest star
And reaches to the lowest hell
The guilty pair, bowed down with care
God gave His Son to win
His erring child He reconciled
And pardoned from his sin.

OH LOVE OF GOD, how rich and pure!
How measureless and strong!
It shall forevermore endure
The saints' and angels' song.

(Song Fragment)

EARTH'S FACE IN DEVASTATION

THE BIBLE IS LIKE A JIGSAW PUZZLE. Until the various pieces of the puzzle are put properly together, the true picture does not emerge. So now let's understand the background (Genesis 1:1). God created the heavens and the earth. The heavens, or universe, and the earth were created after the angels. Earth's angels had not completed the creation of the earth by improvement, development and beautification. Rather they brought it to desolation and ruin. The government of God was nullified on earth.

Lucifer had been stationed at the very throne of God. He was trained and experienced in the administration of the government of God. God chose such a being, well-experienced and trained to oversee the government of God over the angels who inhabited the whole earth. This is not talking about any human beings.

> **"You were blameless in your ways from the day you were created till wickedness was found in you." (Ezekiel 28:15).**

He had complete knowledge, understanding and wisdom. He also was given full powers of reasoning, thinking, making decisions, and making choices. This super being, the highest that even God could create, turned to rebellion against his maker, he turned to lawlessness.

My God We Will Perish

He had been trained in the administration of perfect law and order. As long as Lucifer continued in this perfect way, there was to be happiness and unspeakable joy over the whole earth.

What caused the angels on earth to sin, to turn to lawlessness? Certainly, the ordinary angels did not persuade this great super being to turn traitor. No, it was in him that iniquity was found. After how long? We don't know. God does not really know that! It could have been any numbers of years, from one or less to millions times millions.

But first, before coming to man, we need to fill in the prehistory portion. How did this sin of the angels come to take place? How did it start? Remember that God, the Creator, improves and enhances what He creates by His government. What God creates is to be used. This earth was to be inhabited and used by angels, originally, when God placed, apparently a third of all angels (Revelation 12:4), on the newly-created, perfect, beautiful and glorious earth. God sent the angels over, including Lucifer to administer the government of God. There were only two other beings of this extremely high rank of cherubs, Michael and Gabriel.

From that point, the thought returns to man. King Lucifer was the supreme masterpiece of God's creative power as an individual being created, a monster being that wanted to destroy his own maker, and assume all His power to rule the whole universe.

WHAT MAN HAS DONE

LUCIFER AND HIS ANGELS rebelled and did harmony for their own world to their likeness. He turned the harmonious activity into competition, evil, rebellion and destruction, and into darkness, wastefulness, decay and ruin. Man was placed on earth to restore God's government.

What happened? Perhaps five hundred years later, Adam too disobeyed God. We know about Adam and Eve, how she came to be. We know about the forbidden tree of good and evil.

> "And the LORD God commanded the man, 'You are free to eat from any tree in the garden; but you must not eat from the tree of the knowledge of good and evil, for when you eat from it you will certainly die.'" (Genesis 2:16-17).

And so it did happen, that both Adam and Eve did eat of the forbidden tree, and their eyes were opened to their knowledge, and both committed sin, and sin entered the world. Adam and Eve tried to hide from God. God was very angry for the sin they had done and put an enmity on them, driving them out of the Garden of Eden, Paradise. Lucifer became Satan. Adam lived to be 930 years and died.

My God We Will Perish

At this point we already know about Cain and Abel, how Cain, the first born child on earth, murdered his brother Abel for evil reasons. We know about Noah and his three sons (Shem, light complexion), Ham (black complexion and father of all Black generations), and Japheth (father of all the Asiatic people). We also know about the Tower of Babel, how all three generations were building it, and how God intervened and stopped the construction by confusing their language.

Adam had been created with the potential to be born a son of God, though not yet as a begotten son of God's family. Rather, because of his sin, he became spiritually the property of Satan. He actually chose the law of the evil government, the law of vanity and self-glory. All humanity originated from Adam and Eve. The present world was founded in them. The world has ever since been held captive. God, our heavenly Father, will not forget Adam. He will pay the ransom price, and even yet bring His potential children back to Him through Jesus Christ. Because of Adam's sin, God closed off the tree of life to the world as a whole until the Second Adam, Jesus Christ, shall have deposed Satan and taken over the throne of the earth. There cannot be a law without a penalty. The penalty of human sin is death. The penalty of death has passed Adam and all his children. That penalty had to be paid. So what has man really done on earth where God has placed us? Man has made it ugly, polluted, defiled, and profaned everything his hands have touched. He has polluted the air, and befouled the water in the rivers, lakes and seas. He has deteriorated the land, denuded the forests, thus altering rainfall, and causing the expansion of deserts. He has worn out the soil by neglecting to give it its Sabbath rest every seven years. Man has built cities and allowed them to deteriorate into slums, filth and squalor. All because the very first human rejected God and turned from Him, relying solely on himself, and all Adam's children have done likewise. Man not only ruined the earth, but has destroyed his own health by wrong living, as well as degraded and perverted his own spiritual character.

THE PRINCE OF DARKNESS

SOME OF US like to believe that our planet earth is only millions and millions of years old. I do not agree. I like to say they are wrong. I like to say our world we live in today is billions of years old. About five billion years instead. We don't have to go no further than Genesis 1:1 in our Holy Bible. This verse reads,

"In the beginning God created the heavens and the earth."

So we know it was God who started everything in our solar system. But look carefully, the first sentence of verse 2 reads,

"And the earth was without form, and void; and darkness was upon the face of the deep." (KJV).

So something happened in between. Whatever it is, it refers to God doing something. God needed time, a lot more time to do His project here on earth.

Let's forget the heavens for a moment, even though the heavens and the earth started out at the same time. Let us concentrate on earth first. After all, earth is where we are living right now. And again, this is our subject. Let's concentrate on the last part of Genesis 1:2 ("... and the earth was without form, and void..."). What does this really mean? Then the verse says that "...and darkness was upon the face of the deep." What are we looking at? It seems that in real time, it took lots of extra time, possibly in the billions of years, from verse one to verse two. Let me explain.

God had it all planned out in advance and figured out to His liking, to do something so special, enormous and huge, but then learned that the earth was without form, void and in darkness, something must have happened. Something was delayed, lacking, something was missing, something very important. It's sort of a mystery, a myth perhaps. It sounds like somebody was not doing their job. Yes, God had somebody paying close attention for His purpose of anticipating any approaching danger or opportunity. So what are these myths... angels?

So we know God created angels firsthand before He went on with His creation of the heavens and earth in advance of achieving His objectives. His plans about angels must have been in the hundreds of thousands of angels, if not millions, because God is going to need all of them, all of His angels. God also was going to need special angels to run the universe. God picked three special angels to manipulate and direct His project in mind. He picked Lucifer, Michael and Gabriel. God gave each of them authority to do His work. Of all the angels God created, He gave one-third of them to each elected angel in charge. God assigned Lucifer to supervise His task on earth, and entrusted him one-third of His angels to roam the world.

Here is where the revolution began. Here is where the mystery puzzlement started. Lucifer became greedy and selfish, desiring a much more eager position and wanting to be like God. Lucifer didn't see eye to eye with God's universal plan. Lucifer and his third of angels here

The Prince of Darkness

on earth rebelled against God's authority, and became rebellious, and there was war in heaven.

Lucifer and his army of evil angels led by him, took supreme personification of evil ruler of hell. This explains why in Genesis 1:2 the earth was without form, void and in darkness. Because Lucifer broke off and ceased to cooperate with his assigned duties on earth. This negligence prolonged the earth to a longer time in the making perhaps by billions of years before being finally completed. Lucifer lost his title with God. He is the Prince of Darkness, he is now Satan. He and one-third of his angels were driven out from heaven. He is now an outcast of God. Satan and his evil angels are dwelling on earth. Because he is full of evil and jealousy, he wants to hurt God in any which way he can.

In Genesis 2:7 we read that God replaced Satan and his evil angels with human beings, and by creating man in His own image. He created man, and much later a female for companionship. Human beings and angels are not the same. Angels can move around swiftly while human beings are more soft and steady because they have human flesh.

Because Adam was made of dust, he is subject to God in all aspects. Man's primary role is to be obedient to God as the highest in rank and authority on earth, submissive to his creator in all respect, and most importantly to reject immoral conducts that offend Him. Sin! God put man in the Garden of Eden to tend it and keep it. The Garden of Eden is believed to be in the Middle East around modern-day Assyria, where four riverheads, including the Euphrates River, enrich and fertilize the land, and has an abundance of gold without being excessive. Naturally, Satan being selfish, jealous, crafty, deceptive, evil and mean, and knowing very well that he has been replaced by human beings, uses his power to deceive and bluff man to cause him to disobey God. In an innocent and wicked way, man of flesh and blood, fell in temptation and committed a very grave sin against God's instructions. As a consequence, there was agony and horror for him. He was condemned and punished for his sin.

For disobeying God, man and his wife were driven out of the Garden of Eden to strike on their own. Not only that, their punishment was extremely severe, as they were no longer in the presence of God anymore. Man and woman would now know death. They would die as their reward, and then rest.

In the meantime, remember, God is love, He loves all human beings on this earth. In 2019's world, there are more than seven billion* human beings on the planet. God looks after every one of us, and protects us from Satan, the devil.

Based on February 2019 data from World Population Review.

HE WANTS US GOOD

GOD MADE US GOOD, but we didn't stay good. Remember the story of Adam. He did bad, and after that it was very easy for all men and women to do bad too. Now, God didn't stop with just making this world; He went on hoping that He had His thoughts right. He also made a beautiful heaven. It has everything we need to make us happy, and nothing in it makes us sad. God made heaven for people, but also made hell. He made it bad. In fact, He made it as bad as it could possibly be so that no one would want to go there, so people would try very hard not to go there. However, people still disobey God's commandments, and His desire for them to be good.

From time to time there were people who wanted to be good and do what God told them. So when God would find people like that, He would talk to them, help them, and sometimes God even felt it was very important to take good people away from the bad people. It's very easy for even good people to be followers of bad people. God knows that. So sometimes, we read in the Bible He took the good people away from the bad place where they lived, like He did with Abraham when He pulled him away from the city of Ur. He did the same with Noah and his family when He had them build the ark. He sent the flood of water to save Noah and his family from the evil around them.

My God We Will Perish

If Noah had stayed with the bad people, his family might have soon become bad too.

Sometimes God used other ways. There were many good people and bad people mixed in with them. Well, God knows that if bad people were allowed to stay there and do their wrong things, then it would not be long until other people would be doing the same wrong things too. So God took the bad people away. Like the big earthquake that swallowed people during Korah's rebellion against Moses described in Numbers 16. Yes, they were killed. That was the way God could be sure that they wouldn't spread their evil, their bad behavior to others.

God didn't really kill the bad people because He hated them or lost His temper. Instead, He hated the sinful things they did, the way they lived. God destroyed them so that they wouldn't destroy others, so others wouldn't learn their bad ways too.

THE LANGUAGE WE SPEAK

LANGUAGE DOESN'T JUST EXPRESS THOUGHTS; it can also influence them. Jeremiah 17:9 shows that since mankind yields top Satan's attitudes, the human heart or intellect is "deceitful" and "wicked." And since the human heart is wicked, the thoughts and words that people speak are evil (Matthew 12:34-35).

For the next 1,700 years after Adam and Eve yielded to Satan's corrosive influence, all of humanity continued to speak, and to increasingly corrupt this same original language (Genesis 11:1).

Note that at the end of that era the whole earth was still of one common language. Everyone was still speaking the language God have given Adam, but it had become rife with corruption, reflecting in evil thoughts and actions.

The main population gathered at this time somewhere in the area that is now Iraq, and began collaborating on a huge project motivated by an evil purpose. Two generations earlier, a flood had punished the world's population for its sins. But now humans began to build a tower in which they thought they could survive such punishment, live as they pleased, reject God's authority and law, just as Adam and Eve had, and still avoid the punishment (Genesis 11:2-4). The Tower of Babel was a type of humanity's attitude toward God through our history.

My God We Will Perish

In response, God did something ingenious. He took the gift of a common language, the ability to share and unify thoughts, and abruptly divided it. This immediately divided the people into separate groups. That day God created perhaps dozens of language groups as He "confounded their language," so they were unable to understand one another's speech (Genesis 11:7). This was the origin of the parent language that has resulted in the 6,700 languages spoken today.

That did not result in people repenting to God, but it did slow their project of open rebellion toward God that would have quickly led to self-destruction. Generation after generation, mankind corrupted those languages more and more, bringing us to the present with each one filled with perversions, vulgarities, and impurities.

However, the Bible shows that there is a time in the horizon when languages will be purified and unified once again. The Bible is clear that Jesus Christ will soon return to earth and use God's Holy Spirit and His government to reeducate mankind to love His law and the earth into the "wonderful world of tomorrow."

> "It is written: 'As surely as I live,' says the Lord, 'every knee will bow before me; every tongue will acknowledge God.'" (Romans 14:11).

> "She gave birth to a son, a male child, who 'will rule all the nations with an iron scepter.' And her child was snatched up to God and to his throne." (Revelation 12:5).

> "Coming out of his mouth is a sharp sword with which to strike down the nations. 'He will rule them with an iron scepter.' He treads the winepress of the fury of the wrath of God Almighty. On his robe and on his thigh he has this name written: KING OF KINGS AND LORD OF LORDS." (Revelation 19:15-16).

HOPE

LIVING A LIFE OF HOPE is to believe in the future. It gives us encouragement for an outcome. We feel comfortable and full of confidence knowing that promises and cheers await us in a favorable way. Hope is something we look forward to in our everyday life as we plan our destiny.

We have the hope that our Lord Jesus Christ is coming soon again, a second time to bring us salvation. This hope is in our heart and it will always exist. It's in our mind, our lips, and in our mouth.

We use the word hope meaningfully. In some way, we use it in an awkward way and for convenience only. But let us not forget that the word hope was born when Adam and Eve first sinned. Ever since then, we hope for a better life ahead with Jesus Christ at our door.

> "Praise be to the God and Father of our Lord Jesus Christ! In his great mercy he has given us new birth into a living hope through the resurrection of Jesus Christ from the dead, and into an inheritance that can never perish, spoil or fade. This inheritance is kept in heaven for you, who through faith are shielded by God's power until the coming of the salvation that is ready to be revealed in the last time." (1 Peter 1:3-5).

www.ingramcontent.com/pod-product-compliance
Lightning Source LLC
Chambersburg PA
CBHW022109040426
42451CB00007B/188